ATLAS OF ANIMALS

Created by Gallimard Jeunesse,
Claude Delafosse,
and René Mettler
Illustrated by René Mettler

A FIRST DISCOVERY BOOK

Note: Atlas of Animals is a child's very first atlas.
Using simplified maps, bright illustrations, and basic
information, it introduces young children to the
diversity of animals all over the world.

Cartwheel ·B·O·O·K·S· ®

SCHOLASTIC INC.
New York   Toronto   London   Auckland   Sydney

North America

The bald eagle is the national symbol of the United States.

The skunk is found in Canada, the United States, and northern Mexico.

A raccoon's tail may grow as long as fifteen inches. The raccoon's claws are sharp and strong.

The bison, or buffalo, weighs about two thousand pounds. To get that big, it eats a lot of grass!

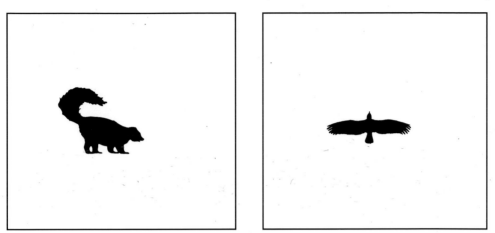

When threatened, the skunk
sprays a bad-smelling liquid
called musk on its enemies.

The eagle's wingspan can
be as long as seven feet.

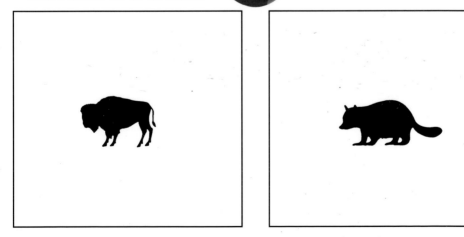

Native Americans used
the skin of the bison to make
tepees and clothes.

Raccoons eat crabs, fish, frogs,
birds' eggs, fruit, nuts, seeds,
grasshoppers, and mice.

South America

The condor of the Andes is a powerful, graceful flier with a wingspan of about ten feet.

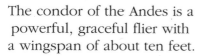

The toco toucan nests in hollow trees in tropical forests from Guyana to Argentina.

The llama is a member of the camel family, even though it has no hump.

The anteater walks on its knuckles to protect its sharp claws.

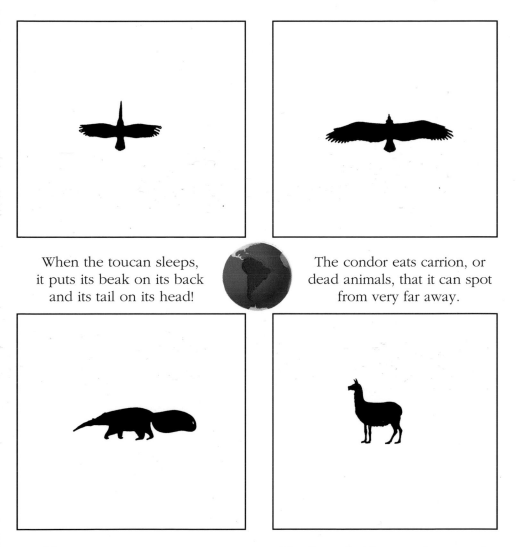

When the toucan sleeps, it puts its beak on its back and its tail on its head!

The condor eats carrion, or dead animals, that it can spot from very far away.

The anteater tears apart ant nests and feeds on ants with its long tongue.

The llama is often used as a pack animal on mountain trails. It can carry about 130 pounds.

South America

The anaconda is more than fifteen feet long. It wraps itself tightly around its prey to kill it.

Only ten inches long, the cotton-top marmoset is one of the world's smallest monkeys.

The sloth moves very slowly. It can sleep hanging from a branch because its claws lock closed.

The tiny hummingbird flies in place as it drinks the nectar from a flower with its long bill.

Southern Asia

The great hornbill is over forty inches long, and makes lots of noise.

The babirusa is a wild hog that lives in Indonesia. It eats mostly fruit and grass.

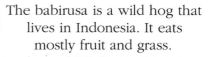

When threatened, the cobra flattens its neck into a hood.

Can you find the phasmid? It is an insect that looks a lot like the branches it sits on.

Southern Asia

The tiger lives in the jungles and bamboo forests of India. It usually hunts at night.

The rhinoceros is one of the largest land creatures. It weighs about two tons!

The giant panda weighs about 330 pounds. It eats bamboo leaves and shoots.

The orangutan uses its long arms to swing from trees in the tropical forests of Sumatra and Borneo.

The rhinoceros used to be hunted for its horn, but now it is protected from hunters.

The tiger eats antelopes, wild boars, and small animals such as monkeys and frogs.

The orangutan is a large, rare ape that eats fruit, leaves, bark, and birds' eggs.

The panda is a very rare animal. It is found only in the mountains of China.

Northern Asia

The saiga, a Siberian antelope, has a keen sense of smell.

The camel's humps store fat, which helps it go up to twelve days without food or water.

Wolves travel in packs in Northern Asia as well as other parts of the world.

The red-breasted goose lives on the tundra. It is a rare bird.

Europe

The ladybug is a small beetle. Ladybugs help fruit growers by eating aphids and other insects.

The swallow travels thousands of miles to avoid cold weather and to find food.

The collared grass snake is a very good swimmer. It is not poisonous.

The female colvert duck pulls out her breast feathers to line her nest. The feathers soon grow back.

Europe

The marmot lives in mountains or on the plains. It is related to the squirrel.

The badger is an expert digger. It digs an underground burrow to live in.

The fox's den may be in a hollow log or tree, a cave, or under the ground.

The red squirrel loves to eat pinecones, which it cuts with its teeth.

Badgers usually hunt at night. They use their claws and teeth as weapons.

The marmot warns its companions by whistling as soon as it senses danger!

By wintertime, the squirrel may have stored up to ten bushels of pinecones!

Foxes are excellent hunters because they are quiet and quick! They hunt rodents.

Africa

The gorilla builds its shelter in the rain forest of central Africa.

The elephant lives in the grassland and the bush, where it eats grass and leaves.

The hippopotamus spends much of its time in lakes and rivers.

The lion rules over the grassland and desert. It hunts zebras and antelopes.

Before it was protected, the elephant was hunted for its ivory tusks.

The gorilla scares away its enemies by pounding on its chest with its fists.

Male lions, like this one, have thick manes of hair. Lions can run up to 35 miles per hour.

The hippopotamus is the third-largest land animal. It eats 130 pounds of vegetation a day.

Africa

Crocodiles have powerful tails to push themselves through the water.

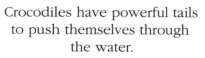

The five-foot-tall marabou stork eats frogs, fish, and reptiles.

The zebra lives in the grassland. In tall grass, the stripes hide the zebra from its enemies.

The okapi is related to the giraffe. It lives in the rain forests of the African country of Zaire.

Africa

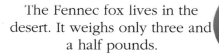

The Fennec fox lives in the desert. It weighs only three and a half pounds.

The one-humped camel, or dromedary, can go six days without water.

The horned viper is able to hide in the sand with only its nostrils and eyes showing.

The oryx is a type of antelope. It is rare because it has long been hunted for its horns.

Australia and Oceania

The mother kangaroo keeps her baby in her pouch for about six months.

The duck-billed platypus uses its flat tail to steer itself while swimming.

Koalas eat eucalyptus leaves. A baby koala rides its mother's back until it is about six months old.

The cockatoo loves the forest but also makes a great pet. It eats nuts, seeds, and fruits.

The Oceans

The colorful angelfish can be found swimming among coral reefs.

The great white shark catches prey by trapping it in its mouth with its sharp teeth.

The blue whale is the largest animal in the world. It can grow up to one hundred feet long!

The octopus swims by sucking water into its body and then pumping it back out.

The Arctic (surrounds the North Pole)

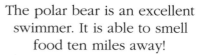

Some arctic terns travel 22,000 miles in a year—to Antarctica and back!

The polar bear is an excellent swimmer. It is able to smell food ten miles away!

The musk ox eats vegetation of the tundra in northern Canada, Alaska, and Greenland.

Baby harp seals of Newfoundland have soft white fur, which they shed weeks after birth.

Antarctica (surrounds the South Pole)

This male emperor penguin is keeping an egg warm on his feet, under his belly.

The arctic tern eats fish and insects. It lays one to three eggs in May or June.

A Weddell seal can dive as deep as 2,360 feet and is able to stay underwater for 45 minutes!

The rock-hopper penguin moves by hopping on both feet!

Find these animals on a page in this book
with other animals that live on the same continent.

NORTH
AMERICA

SOUTH
AMERICA

The African
elephant is
the largest
land animal.

The giant panda
is one of the
rarest animals
in the world.

THE ARCTIC

EUROPE (NORTHERN) ASIA

AFRICA

(SOUTHERN) ASIA

AUSTRALIA

◀ANTARCTICA

The emperor penguin raises its young in the coldest part of the world.

The hummingbird is the smallest bird.

Titles in the series of *First Discovery Books:*

**Airplanes
    and Flying Machines**
All About Time
Bears
*Birds
*Boats
*The Camera
**Cars and Trucks
    and Other Vehicles**
*Castles
Cats
Colors
Dinosaurs
The Earth and Sky
**The Egg

Flowers
Fruit
**The Ladybug and
    Other Insects**
Light
Musical Instruments
Pyramids
The Rain Forest
*The River
The Seashore
**The Tree
Under the Ground
**Vegetables in the
    Garden**
Water
***Weather
*Whales

Titles in the series of
*First Discovery
Art Books:*

Animals
Landscapes
Paintings
Portraits

Titles in the series of
*First Discovery
Atlas Books:*

Atlas of Animals
Atlas of Countries
Atlas of People
Atlas of Plants

Parents Magazine
"Best Books" Award

**Parenting Magazine*
Reading Magic Award

****Oppenheim Toy Portfolio*
Gold Seal Award

Library of Congress Cataloging-in-Publication Data available.

Originally published in France under the title *Atlas des animaux* by Editions Gallimard.

No part of this publication may be reproduced in whole or in part, or stored in a retrieval system, or transmitted in any form or by any means, electronic, mechanical, photocopying, recording, or otherwise, without written permission of the publisher. For information regarding permission, write to Scholastic Inc., 555 Broadway, New York, NY 10012.

ISBN 0-590-58280-1

Copyright © 1994 by Editions Gallimard.
This edition English translation by Jennifer Riggs.
All rights reserved. Published by Scholastic Inc., 555 Broadway, New York, NY 10012 by arrangement with Editions Gallimard•Jeunesse, 5 rue Sebastien-Bottin, F-75007, Paris, France.

CARTWHEEL BOOKS and the CARTWHEEL BOOKS logo are registered trademarks of Scholastic Inc.

12 11 10 9 8 7 6 5 4 3 2 1   6 7 8 9/9 0/0

Printed in Italy by Editoriale Libraria
First Scholastic printing, March 1996